by Dermot McManus
illustrated by Eileen Hine

HOUGHTON MIFFLIN BOSTON

Printed in Mexico

ISBN-13: 978-0-547-02826-2
ISBN-10: 0-547-02826-1

2 3 4 5 6 7 8 9 0908 15 14 13 12 11 10 09

Bear liked to talk. Bear talked about the sky and the snow. He talked about the lake and the trees.

But most of all, Bear loved to talk about his long, brown tail.

Bear was very proud of his tail. "Bears have the best tails," he told Fox. "Fox tails are too short."

Fox was tired of hearing Bear brag about his tail.

One winter day, Bear saw Fox eating a fish near the lake.

"That fish looks good, Fox!" said Bear. He waved his furry tail. "How did you catch it? The lake is covered with ice."

Fox watched Bear wave his long tail. He thought about the times Bear bragged about his tail. He thought about the times Bear said that fox tails were too short.

Then Fox thought of a trick to play on Bear.

"I caught this nice fish with my tail," Fox told Bear. "I made a hole in the ice and put my tail in the hole."

"I will do that, too!" cried Bear. "My tail is longer than yours. I will catch many fish with my tail."

Bear made a hole in the ice and put his tail in the hole. Bear sat on the ice for a long time.

He kept his tail in the cold water, but he didn't catch any fish. Bear felt cold and hungry.

At last, Bear knew Fox had tricked him. Bear was angry. He yanked his long tail from the water.

But his tail had frozen in the icy lake, and it snapped right off!

Bear was sad. He missed his long furry tail.

He learned a lesson that day. Nobody likes a bear who brags!

Responding

TARGET SKILL **Sequence of Events** What happened first in the story? What happened next? What happened last? Make a chart.

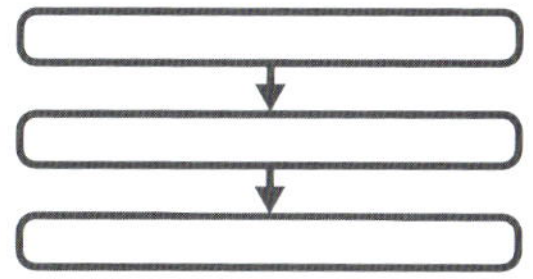

Write About It

Text to Text Think of a different story that tells why an animal looks the way it looks. Draw a picture of the animal. Write a sentence to tell about the animal.

WORDS TO KNOW

been	off
brown	out
know	own
never	very

TARGET SKILL **Sequence of Events** Tell the order in which things happen.

TARGET STRATEGY **Question** Ask questions about what you are reading.

GENRE A **folktale** is a story that is often told by people of a country.